Copyright © 2024 by Bridget K. Lambright

All rights reserved. No part of this publication may be reproduced, distributed, or transmitted in any form or by any means, including photocopying, recording, or other electronic or mechanical methods, without the prior written permission of the publisher, except in the case of brief quotations embodied in critical reviews and certain other noncommercial uses permitted by copyright law. For permission requests, email the publisher at teentiptip@gmail.com.

Ordering Information:
Quantity sales. Special discounts are available on quantity purchases by schools, corporations, associations, and others. For details, contact the publisher at the website above.

Printed in the United States of America

ISBN 978-0-9796578-6-3

Hello,

These pages reveal secrets that most adults don't want you to know. As a child, I tended to only see the best in grown-ups. I was raised to give them the benefit of the doubt.

Big mistake!

Now, I'm an old lady who has been observing way too much foolishness in far too many places. Adults can be so weird or downright harmful. I understand why so many young people are shutting down or feeling hopeless. This coloring book is exposing the reality of how lots of adults, myself included, misbehave.

Knowledge is power.

Your perception of how you're being treated matters. When dealing with grown-ups in schools, offices, stores, restaurants, courts, churches, hospitals, neighborhoods, etc., it helps to recognize our personalities. Protect yourself accordingly. Millions of us aren't interested in changing for your sake...let alone to become better. Please don't allow us to intentionally or unintentionally violate your mind, body, or spirit.

@ 2024 Bridget Lambright-Tommelleo

Spoiler Alert:

There are millions of adults who believe that they have every right to display these harsh personalities because you're just a kid. They will dislike this coloring book. However, my priority is your safety and mental health.

You Matter,

BLT

Personality:

Naysayer

Lots of grown-ups completely believe stereotypes.

How to Handle:
Believe in yourself. Don't let any man/woman limit you. Keep pushing. Prove him/her wrong. Be your best. Tune them out.

Personality:

Bogus

Most adults are only pretending to be nice.

How to Handle:

Pretend to be nice too. Don't trust them too much. Watch your back.

Personality:

Bully

There are countless grown-ups who will use teenagers and little kids as their emotional punching bags on a bad day.

How to Handle:
Tell your parents/guardians. Refuse to be alone with this person. Tell a trusted adult. Tell a supervisor. Send an email to the main office describing a specific incident(s). Secretly record and blast on social media. Contact the news. Don't stop reporting verbally and in writing.

Personality:
Spiteful

Yes, men and women can be jealous of kids.

How to Handle:
Directly inform the adult in front of witnesses that he/she is being harsh and hurting your mental health (without any further explanation). Avoid being alone with this individual. Tell your parents/guardians. Ask a trusted adult to secretly observe your interactions with the adult. Tell a supervisor. Send an email to the main office regarding a specific incident(s). Report snarky comments made after you get help. Don't stop reporting verbally and in writing.

© 2024 Bridget Lambright-Tommelleo

Personality:

Bigot

Plenty of adults work with young people for a salary plus benefits while finding them repulsive.

How to Handle:

Tell your parents/guardians. Tell a trusted adult and supervisor via email. Send an email to the main office regarding a specific incident(s). Ask peers for witness statements. Seek an attorney. Don't stop reporting verbally and in writing.

Personality:

Devious

Grown-ups with degrees and good jobs can still be very bad people.

How to Handle:

Don't trust this person. Watch your back. Tell your parents or guardians.

Personality:
Miserable

Nonstop complaining and blaming is a bad habit for lots of men and women.

How to Handle:
Ignore his/her negativity. Draw funny pictures that depict the ugliness of the person's heart. Inform the person in front of witnesses that he/she is harming the environment with his/her terrible mood. Walk away.

Personality:

Simpleton

Far too many grown-ups will make offensive statements without considering the insulting impact.

How to Handle:
Stay calm. Write down or record what was said. If necessary, request clarification and report. Ignore defiant responses. Tell your parents/guardians. Inform the individual that you're offended. No need to justify yourself. Be on guard. Protect your mental health by avoiding this person. Warn others.

@ 2024 Bridget Lambright-Tommelleo

Personality:

Two-Faced

Every smiling adult isn't friendly.

How to Handle:
Smile EXTRA big back at him/her. Don't trust this person at all. Pretend like you believe he/she is nice. Warn your friends.

Personality:
Ruthless

Some men and women in uniforms don't have a problem with hurting kids.

How to Handle:
Be where you're supposed to be. Do what you're supposed to be doing. Immediately ask for your parents/guardians. Keep calm. Barely talk. Avoid arguing no matter what. Try to record. Pay close attention. Follow his/her directions. Ask witnesses to remain. Obtain their contact information. Immediately submit a request for any unedited video. Contact an attorney. Go to therapy.

Personality:

Con

Too many adults lie all the time.

How to Handle:

Prepare for disappointment. Never give the benefit of the doubt. Watch your back. Require your trust be earned. Keep a record of the lie(s) for future reference. If possible, ALWAYS keep receipts (evidence) handy.

Personality:

Hardened

It's tough to find grown-ups whose deeds match their sweet words.

How to Handle:

Don't let their unhappiness ruin your day. Ignore any sour adult who says mean stuff about sweet people. Always remember that it's 100% their problem and 0% your problem.

Personality:

Tormentor

Millions of adults think it's funny to bash a person's looks, abilities, and needs on social media.

How to Handle:

Report harmful content to the website. Send their hateful screenshots to their employer or Google reviews. Don't trust men and women who savagely mock others.

Personality:

Creepy

More than a few adults find little ones or teens tempting.

How to Handle:

Never-ever be alone with this person. Don't ignore your uncomfortable feeling. Don't believe that it's your fault. Never share pictures or messages. Tell your parents/guardians. Tell your friends. Tell a trusted adult. Call 211 for advice. Tell the main office. Keep all screenshots and recordings. Ask for witness statements. Get a lawyer. Tell the police. Don't stop reporting verbally and in writing. Sue.

Hello again,

By now you're probably noticing two things. First, my design boo-boos in the pictures were left on purpose to make you laugh. Perfection wasn't my goal. Adults aren't perfect. My focus was making sure that you get these tips to keep you from feeling powerless.

Second, I intentionally didn't focus on the not so common personalities in our society. You don't need any protection from these grown-ups. They are selfless, fair, upbeat, humble, polite, sensible, honest, calm, and responsible adults. These grown-ups just naturally make everyone, regardless of where they come from, feel special, loved, respected, smart, safe, heard, and valued. They own their faults, accept accountability, have big hearts, apologize, and are constantly trying to be better people. Their acts of kindness will speak for them. Your heart will tell you that they are good people. Please try to be like them.

© 2024 Bridget Lambright-Tommelleo

Personality:

Mayhem

Argumentative men and women enjoy wrecking everyone's peace.

How to Handle:

Avoid this person as much as possible. Remain silent in his/her presence. Tell a trusted adult. Share evidence of hostility with security.

Personality:

Narcissist

Most men and women are too full of themselves to take responsibility for causing harm.

How to Handle:

Avoid/Ignore this person. Don't believe anything he/she says. Beware of these adults' mind games. Stand up for yourself.

@ 2024 Bridget Lambright-Tommelleo

Personality:

Scornful

Bitter adults wear their bitterness in their cruel eyes and pessimistic body language.

How to Handle:

Ignore their bad energy. Don't let their yucky attitude rub off on you. Draw silly pictures of their mean facial expressions.

Personality:
Monster

Grown-ups with violent tendencies can be vicious towards kids they fear or loathe.

How to Handle:
Directly inform the adult in front of witnesses that he/she is being cruel and hurting your mental health (without any further explanation). Avoid being alone with this individual. Tell your parents/guardians. Ask a trusted adult to secretly observe your interactions with the adult. Tell a supervisor. Send an email to the main office describing a specific incident(s). Don't stop reporting verbally and in writing.

© 2024 Bridget Lambright-Tommelleo

Personality:

Gross

Cleanliness after using the bathroom isn't a priority for quite a few men and women.

How to Handle:

Use tissue or paper towels to open doors. Avoid being at the end of food lines. Use a napkin to pick up public items. Constantly sanitize your hands. Don't accept everyone's treats.

Personality:

Pearl

Crossing paths with wise adults is rare.

How to Handle:

Learn as much as you can from knowledgeable people. Treat good advice like a valuable diamond. Tell your friends to listen too.

Personality:

Thug

Men and women will gang up to crush their opposition.

How to Handle:

Be like David versus Goliath. Give this one to your parents/guardians and an attorney. Send an email to the main office regarding every incident. Don't stop reporting verbally and in writing. Be a squeaky wheel. Spread the word about your suffering to organizations who are connected to these adults. Reach out to the news too.

Personality:

Rude

Grown-ups will demand respect without giving respect.

How to Handle:
Tell your parents/guardians. Try to ignore him/her. Get a trusted adult involved. Avoid arguing because it makes you look bad while the disrespectful adult looks like the victim.

Personality:

Insecure

Only a small number of adults possess sufficient self-confidence to never feel intimidated.

How to Handle:

Avoid these people like a booger on your finger. Ignore any negativity they try to push at you. Tell your parents/guardians. Always remember that it's 100% their problem and 0% your problem. Be unbothered.

Personality:

Needy

Social media is a drug for those pitiful men and women who never achieved fame during high school.

How to Handle:

Don't care. Laugh at their need to be relevant on a computer. Enjoy having youth and more time to be alive on your side.

Personality:

Buffoon

Immature grown-ups repeatedly make a bad situation worse.

How to Handle:

Avoid these folks. Don't be like them. That's all I got.

Personality:

Partial

The countless adults who deny showing favoritism definitely have favorites.

How to Handle:
Tell your parents/guardians. Get a trusted adult involved. Send an email to the main office regarding every incident. Don't stop reporting verbally and in writing. Be a squeaky wheel.

Personality:

Hypocrite

So many grown folks are guilty of doing exactly what they constantly tell kids or other adults not to do.

How to Handle:

Don't be like them. Live your life like someone with standards. Don't trust them. Laugh behind their back.

Personality:

Dull

Lots of adults make hostile gestures because they lack etiquette and self-control.

How to Handle:

Report any incidents to your parents/guardians. Tell a trusted adult. Share your pictures and recordings catching them in the act.

Personality:

Imposter

When nasty men and women get called out for their toxic personality, they'll never admit the truth.

How to Handle:

Avoid these folks. Don't bother trying to convince them. Don't trust them.

Personality:

Divisive

Our society is full of adults who only listen to disagree instead of to understand.

How to Handle:

Avoid these folks too. Don't waste your energy on them. Don't trust them. Watch your back. Tune them out.

PLEASE CHECK OUT MY HIGH SCHOOL READINESS BOOK TO MAKE SURE THAT YOUR PERSONALITY IS ON THE RIGHT TRACK!

WWW.MAXIMIZESCHOOL.COM